ADORABLE ANIMAL BABIES

BABY ANIMALS IN THE SNOW

SARAH RIDLEY

PowerKiDS press

Published in 2026
by The Rosen Publishing Group, Inc.
2544 Clinton Street, Buffalo, NY 14224

First published in Great Britain in 2021 by Wayland

Editor: Nicola Edwards
Designer: Lisa Peacock

Cataloging-in-Publication Data

Names: Ridley, Sarah.
Title: Baby animals in the snow / Sarah Ridley.
Description: Buffalo, NY : PowerKids Press, 2026. | Series: Adorable animal babies | Includes glossary and index.
Identifiers: ISBN 9781499453614 (pbk.) | ISBN 9781499453621 (library bound) | ISBN 9781499453638 (ebook)
Subjects: LCSH: Tundra animals--Infancy--Juvenile literature. | Tundra animals--Juvenile literature.
Classification: LCC QL104.R535 2026 | DDC 591.70911'3--dc23

Manufactured in the United States of America
CPSIA Compliance Information: Batch #CSPK26. For further information contact Rosen Publishing at 1-800-237-9932.

Picture acknowledgements:
FLPA Images: Samuel Blanc/Biosphoto 25b. Nature PL: Eric Baccega 7t, 11b; Stephan Christmann 20, 21,22t; Jasper Doest/Minden 16t; Sergey Gorshkov 5b; Michio Hoshino 13t; Mitsuaki Mac 26t; Dave Watts 24t; Konrad Wothe 27t. Shutterstock: Agami Photo Agency 25t; AndreAnita 6t, 6b; Antarctic 29tl; Bildagentur Zoonar GmbH 29br; 27c Janice Chen; Coulanges 12; Jo Crebbin 9b, 15t; Chase Dekker 18t; Werner Engles 15b, 28tr; Enrique front cover, 10b, 28bl; Evaurban 1, 28tl; Giedriius 5t,16b,17t, 28br; Andrey Gudkov 26b, 27b; Dolores M Harvey 10t, 13b; Mario Hoppmann 23b; Don Mammoser 29tc; Svalbard and Jan Mayen 8t; Polarman 4t; Pole 2 Pole Images 14; Ondrej Prosicky 17b; Rbrown10 9t; Alex Seafearer 7b, 8b; Slowmotiongli 11t; Studio Wing 4b; Tarpan 24b, 29bc, 29tr; Sergey Uryadnikov 18b, 19b; Vladsilver 2,22b, 23t; Wild At Art 19t; Oscar Wistrand 29bl.

CONTENTS

Snow Babies	4
Polar Bear Cubs	6
Seal Pups	10
Walrus Calves	14
Arctic Fox Cubs	16
Grizzly Bear Cubs	18
Penguin Chicks	20
Snow Petrel Chicks	24
Monkey Babies	26
Can You Remember?	28
Glossary	30
Answers	31
Index	32

Words in **bold** are in the glossary on pages 30-31.

SNOW BABIES

It is hard for animals to raise their babies in cold places where there is little food. Many animals travel to somewhere warmer. Others stay and find different ways to care for their young.

Drinking its mother's milk has given this ringed seal **pup** a layer of **blubber** to help keep it warm.

These lynx **cubs** have thick fur to keep them warm. They **depend** on their mother for food until they are about ten months old.

Musk ox **calves** are born in the summer when there is more food to eat. Soon the snow returns. This calf will shelter under its mother's hair to survive winter storms.

In a few minutes, this newborn reindeer calf will stand up and drink milk from its mother. A day later it will be able to run with the **herd** as the reindeer travel in search of plants to eat.

POLAR BEAR CUBS

Polar bears live in the **Arctic**. Four months ago, this female polar bear dug a **den** under the snow and gave birth to cubs. Now it's time to come out for the first time.

When they are born, polar bear cubs are deaf and blind. They drink milk from their mother and grow a little every day. By the time they leave the den, they have thick fur.

For the first two weeks, they stay close to the den. The cubs play and learn how to move on the snow.

Then their mother leads them on a long walk to **hunt** for food. The cubs call to their mother: *maa. Chuff* ... she grunts at them if they are too far away.

The mother is called a sow. She is very hungry as she has not eaten for months. She uses her sense of smell to hunt seals.

For the next two-and-a-half years, the sow will teach her cubs how to hunt and survive. Cubs play fight to learn how to fight later in life.

They learn how to swim, following their mother wherever she goes.

Polar bear cubs continue to drink milk from their mother until they are about 20 months old.

SEAL PUPS

Harp seals live in the Arctic. A female seal is called a cow. Her pup grows inside her for 225 days. When she is ready, she pulls herself onto floating ice, picks a good spot, and gives birth.

A seal pup is covered in fluffy white fur to stay warm and hide from **predators**.

For the next 10 to 12 days, the pup **suckles** from its mother. Her milk is so full of fat that the pup grows fast.

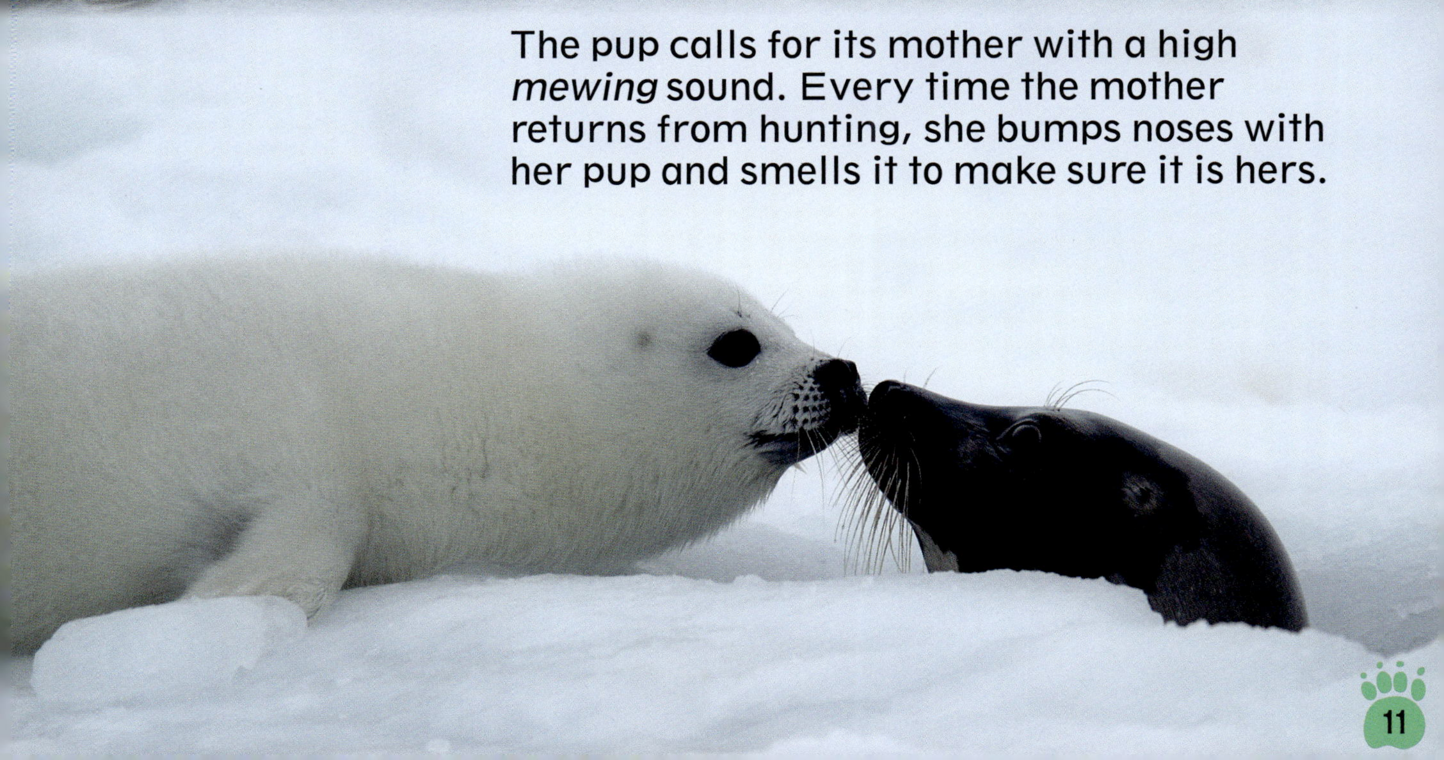

The pup calls for its mother with a high *mewing* sound. Every time the mother returns from hunting, she bumps noses with her pup and smells it to make sure it is hers.

The pup grows fast and will become three times heavier than when it was born!

After about 12 days it is time for the pup to learn to swim. The mother calls, *ark*, and her pup slides into the water where it soon discovers that swimming is easy.

Now the mother knows her pup can swim, she leads it back onto the ice. During the next six weeks the pup's fur changes into thick, waterproof fur. It does not eat during this time. Once its fur is waterproof, the young seal can start hunting fish for itself.

WALRUS CALVES

Another Arctic **mammal** is the walrus. This calf was born on **sea ice**. Mother and calf learn the look of each other's face and **whiskers**. They *bark* at each other.

Walrus calves can swim when they are young. When this calf gets tired, its mother will give it a ride on her back or hold it in a hug. The calf often drinks milk from its mother underwater.

Mother and calf stay close for about three years. In that time, the mother teaches her calf where to search for food and protects it from danger.

ARCTIC FOX CUBS

It is early summer in the Arctic. These Arctic fox cubs were born in an underground den about four weeks ago. At first, they drink their mother's milk. Then they start eating meat as well.

The cubs have dark brown fur which helps hide them from predators. Cubs learn to hunt by playing with each other.

Both parents hunt small animals to feed to their cubs. The cubs need to grow strong before winter.

By winter, the cubs will have grown thick, snow-white fur, like this adult Arctic fox.

GRIZZLY BEAR CUBS

Some grizzly bears live in Canada and Alaska. A mother grizzly bear gives birth in her winter den. Her cubs suckle and sleep next to her until it is time to leave the den about three months later.

Soon the snow melts and bear cubs start exploring. These cubs are learning how to climb trees ...

... and this one is trying out fishing.

Grizzly bear cubs continue to drink their mother's milk for up to three years. These bigger cubs have woken up after another winter sleep with their mother.

PENGUIN CHICKS

Emperor penguins bring up their **chicks** in the coldest place on Earth: The **Antarctic.** In early winter, they pair up. The female lays an egg and gives it to her **mate.** He keeps the egg warm under a fold of skin for the next two months.

All through the long winter, the fathers keep the eggs warm. Then the chicks start to **hatch**! Soon the mothers will return from their long hunting trips out at sea and meet their chicks for the first time.

Peep! The chick is hungry. The parents swap places and the mother brings up a fishy soup from her stomach to feed her chick. Now the hungry father sets off to hunt for food.

The parents take it in turns to keep their chick warm or hunt for food to feed it. They find each other among all the other penguins by calling. They know the sound of their chick's high *peep* as well.

When the parents think their chick is ready, they leave it with other chicks and go hunting together. The chick is growing fast so it is always hungry and needs both parents to feed it.

After about five months, the chick is almost as tall as its parents. Soon it will grow waterproof feathers and start to hunt for itself.

SNOW PETREL CHICKS

Snow petrels bring up their chick together. They take it in turns to keep their egg warm in a rocky place out of the Antarctic wind.

The chick hatches after six or seven weeks. It is covered in gray, **downy** feathers to help keep it warm.

Now the parents spend their days fishing **krill**, fish, and **squid** out of the icy sea. They feed it to their chick as a fishy soup.

The chick's feathers slowly turn white as they change into adult feathers. It *chirrups* when its parents return with food. After about seven weeks the chick can fly and hunt for itself. It could live for up to 20 years.

MONKEY BABIES

High in the mountains of Japan live macaque (say *muh-KAK*) monkeys. The mother gives birth in the summer when the weather is warmer. The baby drinks milk from its mother.

By the time winter arrives, the baby has grown thick fur. It clings to its mother's back as they travel around.

Baby monkeys learn by copying what other monkeys do. This one is making snowballs!

The mother monkey **grooms** her baby to show her love and to keep her baby clean. She teaches it how to find food.

These monkeys live near **hot springs**. The mother has taken her baby into the warm water to warm it up and relax!

CAN YOU REMEMBER?

Now you have read about some snow babies, can you remember their special names?

1.

2.

3.

4.

5.

6.

7.

8.

9.

10.

The answers are on page 31.

GLOSSARY

Antarctic the land and sea around the South Pole

Arctic the land and sea around the North Pole

blubber a layer of fat under the skin of sea mammals that helps keep warm

calf (plural **calves**) the name for the young of many types of animal, including reindeer and walruses

chick the young of a bird

cub the name for the young of many types of animal, including foxes and bears

den the underground or hidden home of some animals

depend to need the help of somebody or something

downy covered with very soft feathers

groom to clean the fur or skin of another animal, or itself

hatch to come out of an egg

herd a group of animals, such as reindeer, that live together

hot springs hot water that bubbles up naturally from deep under the ground

hunt to go after a wild animal to kill it (for food)

krill a tiny shellfish that lives in oceans around the world

mammal any animal that gives birth to live young, has fur, and feeds its young on milk

mate a male or female partner for an animal

predator an animal that eats other animals

pup the name for the young of many types of animal, including seals

sea ice frozen ocean water found at the North Pole and the South Pole

squid an animal with long arms, called tentacles, that lives in the sea

suckle when a baby animal drinks milk from its mother's breast, teat, or udder

whiskers long, stiff hairs growing near the mouth of an animal

Answers
1. polar bear cubs; 2. harp seal pup; 3. walrus calf; 4. arctic fox cubs; 5. emperor penguin chicks; 6. grizzly bear cub; 7. snow petrel chick; 8. baby macaque; 9. reindeer calf; 10. lynx cub.

INDEX

Arctic foxes 16–17, 28

calves 5, 14–15, 28–29
chicks 20–25, 29
cubs 4, 6–9, 16–19, 28–29

grizzly bears 18–19, 29

lynx 4, 29

monkeys 26–27, 29
musk oxen 5

penguins 20–23, 29
polar bears 6–9, 28
pups 4, 10–13, 28

reindeer 5, 29

seals 4, 8, 10–13, 28
snow petrels 24–25, 29

walruses 14–15, 28